CURIOUS CREATURES
COLORING BOOK

Amy Weber

DOVER PUBLICATIONS, INC.
Mineola, New York

NOTE

Ideal for artists of all ages, the playful whimsy of these creative illustrations offer the perfect opportunity to experiment with color. This delightful collection of imaginative renderings features such lively designs as animals in space, pigs on planes, zany creatures under the sea, and adorable little mice made up of steampunk-style gears. Unique and robotic-looking animals present a surreal theme that will inspire budding artists as well as experienced colorists. Rendered by artist Amy Weber, the 31 plates in this book are perforated for easy removal and are printed on one side only.

Copyright
Copyright © 2013 by Amy Weber
All rights reserved.

Bibliographical Note
Creative Haven Curious Creatures Coloring Book is a new work, first published by Dover Publications, Inc., in 2013.

International Standard Book Number
ISBN-13: 978-0-486-49269-8
ISBN-10: 0-486-49269-9

Manufactured in the United States by RR Donnelley
49269908   2015
www.doverpublications.com